Going to Work SCHOOL EDITION · Going to Work SCHOOL EDITION · Going to Work SCHOOL EDITION · Going to
SCHOOL EDITION · Going to Work SCHOOL EDITION · Going to Work SCHOOL EDITION · Going to
CHOOL EDITION · Going to Work SCHOOL EDITION · Going to Work SCHOOL EDITION · Going to
CHOOL EDITION · Going to Work SCHOOL EDITION · Going to Work SCHOOL EDITION · HOOL E

Going To Work
SCHOOL EDITION

Bus Drivers

Buddy BOOKS
Going To Work

ABDO
Publishing Company

A Buddy **Book by**
Julie Murray

VISIT US AT

www.abdopublishing.com

Published by ABDO Publishing Company, 8000 West 78th Street, Edina, Minnesota 55439.

Copyright © 2011 by Abdo Consulting Group, Inc. International copyrights reserved in all countries. No part of this book may be reproduced in any form without written permission from the publisher. Buddy Books™ is a trademark and logo of ABDO Publishing Company.

Printed in the United States of America, North Mankato, Minnesota.
022010
092010

♻ PRINTED ON RECYCLED PAPER

Coordinating Series Editor: Rochelle Baltzer
Editor: Sarah Tieck
Contributing Editors: Heidi M.D. Elston, Megan M. Gunderson, BreAnn Rumsch, Marcia Zappa
Graphic Design: Maria Hosley
Cover Photograph: *Corbis*: ©Andersen Ross/Blend Images.
Interior Photographs/Illustrations: *AP Photo*: Ric Feld (p. 13), Jim Stratakos/The Herald (p. 30), Coke Whitworth (p. 17); *Corbis*: ©Chris Barth/Star Ledger (p. 23), ©William Gottlieb (p. 27), ©moonboard (p. 5), ©Dave Reede/AgStock Images (p. 8); *Getty Images*: FPG/Hulton Archive (p. 25); Michael P. Goecke (pp. 12, 15, 21, 29); *iStockphoto*: ©iStockphoto.com/halbergman (p. 11), ©iStockphoto.com/LeggNet (p. 7), ©iStockphoto.com/Zeiss4Me (p. 21); *Photolibrary.com*: Stockbyte (p. 19); *Shutterstock*: carroteater (p. 17), Morgan Lane Photography (p. 9).

Library of Congress Cataloging-in-Publication Data

Murray, Julie, 1969-
  Bus drivers / Julie Murray.
    p. cm. -- (Going to work : school edition)
  ISBN 978-1-61613-504-1
  1. School buses--Juvenile literature. 2. Bus drivers--Juvenile literature. 3. School children--Transportation--Juvenile literature. I. Title.
  LB2864.M87 2011
  371.8'72--dc22
                                                              2009050819

Contents

People at Work

Going to work is an important part of life. At work, people use their skills to complete tasks and earn money.

There are many different types of workplaces. Schools, factories, and offices are all workplaces.

Some bus drivers drive students to and from school. Their work is important to student safety and the school day.

School bus drivers are caring and helpful.

Driver's Seat

School bus drivers spend their time behind the wheel of a school bus. Most work part-time.

School bus drivers mostly work before and after the school day. But some have midday kindergarten bus **routes**. Others drive students and teachers to special events or field trips.

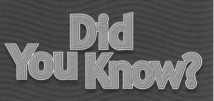

Some school bus drivers also work part-time in schools. They often work as janitors, mechanics, or classroom helpers.

Many students depend on bus drivers to get them to school safely.

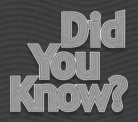
Did You Know?

About 480,000 U.S. school buses take 26 million children to and from school each day.

Students of all ages ride school buses. On average, 30 to 40 students ride a bus at the same time.

Students follow the same rules on a school bus as in a classroom. Some buses have student monitors who make sure rules are followed. Rules help protect every rider.

Students may have assigned seats on their school bus. This helps keep their ride safe and orderly.

Driving Work

To become a bus driver, a person must have a driver's **license**. He or she must also have a good driving record. And usually, a school bus driver has completed high school.

Bus drivers take driving and written tests. They get special driver's licenses. These prove they can drive large buses with many riders.

A driver's license is a small card. A driver is expected to carry it while driving. It usually shows his or her picture.

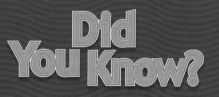

Driver's licenses look different in each state.

Did You Know?

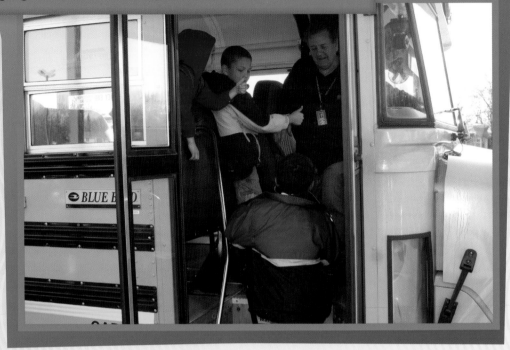

Being a good listener is an important job skill for bus drivers.

Bus drivers often must pass tests at a doctor's office. These tests make sure drivers are healthy and strong.

Bus drivers also get background checks. These prove they are trustworthy and follow the law.

Students should check both ways for cars before and after getting off the bus.

Job Training

After they are hired, school bus drivers receive job training. They learn how to care for buses and **manage** large groups of students. They also learn about safety and how to handle **emergencies**.

During training, school bus drivers practice turning corners and backing up. They also learn to use special controls. Some drivers learn how to operate a wheelchair lift.

Buses have special tools on board to help drivers. First aid kits (*above right*) help treat small injuries. Radios (*above*) allow drivers to talk to one another. Mirrors (*right*) help drivers see the road.

A Day at Work

Most school bus drivers begin work early in the morning. After they start the bus engine, they do a safety check. They walk around the bus to see that it is working properly. They make sure the lights are on and the tires are filled with air.

When they know the bus is safe, school bus drivers begin their first **route**. Many drive more than one route each day. They also drive routes after school.

16

School buses are large and brightly colored.
This makes them easy for other drivers to see.

Drivers take care of their buses.
This includes filling them with fuel.

Safe and Trusted

Buses are among the safest vehicles on the road. They are very large. Their size helps bus drivers easily see the road. And, it **protects** riders in a crash.

Most buses do not have seat belts. This is because bus seats are designed for safety. Still, some people want to add seat belts to buses. They feel this will make buses safer for students.

School bus seats are strong. They surround students with high backs and padding for safety. These features protect students like egg cartons protect eggs.

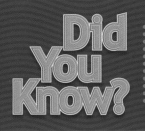

Did You Know?

Students must be prepared to exit buses safely during emergencies. Schools hold drills so they can practice.

Bus drivers are well trained. They must be ready for anything, including bad weather. Bus drivers also need to pay close attention to other cars on the road. School bus drivers do their best to **protect** students. Students must do their part by behaving safely. It is everyone's job to follow bus safety rules.

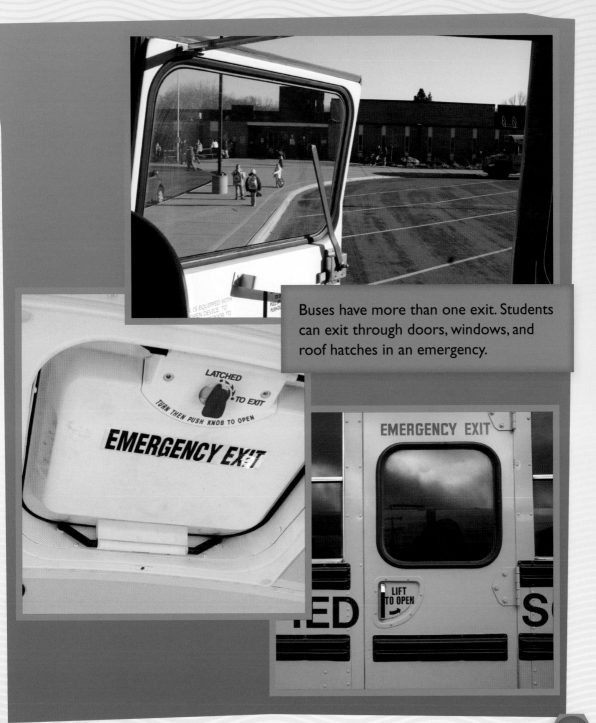

Buses have more than one exit. Students can exit through doors, windows, and roof hatches in an emergency.

Special Trips

Sometimes, teachers and students leave school for special events and activities. They may go on field trips or attend school sporting events. School bus drivers take them where they need to go.

Field trips and sporting events may take place at night or on weekends. So, school bus drivers sometimes work after their regular routes.

HISTORY LESSON

Since the start of public schools, students have traveled together to classes. Before there were cars and buses, students walked or biked to school. Others rode in horse-drawn carts.

In the 1920s, cars, trucks, and buses began to replace horse-drawn carts. This was the beginning of the modern-day school bus.

Years ago, school buses looked very different!

Early school buses had safety problems. So in 1939, U.S. school bus standards were created.

Over the years, more safety standards were added. Buses must now have rearview mirrors, red warning lights, stop signs, and **emergency** exits.

Starting in 1939, school buses were painted a special yellow color. This helps people easily see them, especially in the early morning light.

Helpful Workers

School bus drivers have an important job. They safely drive students and teachers. School bus drivers do special work that benefits the community!

Better buses, standards, and training have improved school bus safety over the years.

The School News

Using Computers

Computers help plan bus **routes**. They plan each turn for drivers. And, they figure out each route's time and length.

Yellow is Green

School buses help **protect** Earth. When students ride together on a bus, it saves fuel and creates less pollution. Some buses even run on electricity! They get plugged in to recharge.

Important Words

emergency (ih-MUHR-juhnt-see) an unexpected event that requires immediate action.

license (LEYE-suhnts) a paper or a card showing that someone is allowed to do something by law.

manage to look after or make decisions about.

monitor a person who watches, keeps track of, or oversees something.

protect (pruh-TEHKT) to guard against harm or danger.

route (ROOT) a regular, chosen way to travel.

Web Sites

To learn more about bus drivers, visit ABDO Publishing Company online. Web sites about bus drivers are featured on our Book Links page. These links are routinely monitored and updated to provide the most current information available.

www.abdopublishing.com

Index

32